THE Spanish Armada

PROJECT BOOK

David McDowall

Project Consultant: Valerie Nott

HODDER AND STOUGHTON
LONDON SYDNEY AUCKLAND TORONTO

Clash of titans

Early one Sunday morning in the summer of 1588, the Spanish Armada and the English fleet faced each other for battle, off Plymouth. It was the moment all Europe had been waiting for. The Spanish Armada was the largest fleet ever assembled, totalling 130 ships. Everyone knew its mission: to overthrow Queen Elizabeth, and to make England Catholic again.

On the decks of the Spanish ships stood finely dressed noblemen and uniformed soldiers, their helmets and breastplates glistening in the sun. At the mastheads flew colourful flags, some with coats of arms, others of red and yellow stripes, the national colours of Spain. Some of the sails were painted, too, with the Spanish royal coat of arms, or with religious symbols. It was a brave sight.

Pitted against the Spanish Armada was the best and biggest navy England had ever built. It was divided into two fleets, the main one, 90 ships strong, now faced the Armada. A smaller fleet of 40 ships stood guard in the Straits of Dover, at the other end of the English Channel. The English, too, made a colourful show, with flags and banners fluttering bravely in the breeze. But on the decks there bustled more sailors, and few finely dressed noblemen or soldiers.

Everyone knew that the fate of England would be decided in the next few days, and if England was defeated, Catholic Spain would probably go on to defeat the Protestants of Europe too.

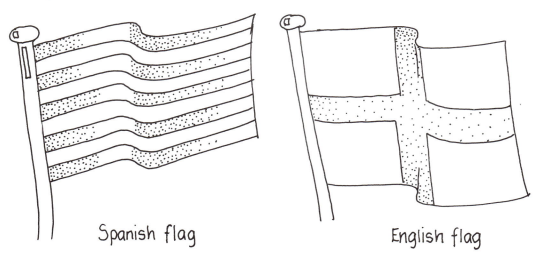

Spanish flag English flag

Everyone also knew that the outcome would depend on:

1 the winds and tides in the Channel
2 the fleet with the better seamanship
3 the fleet with the better fighting skills.

Expecting the English fleet to attack at any moment, the Spanish admiral fired his signal gun. Immediately the great Armada formed battle order, the gun ports were opened, and the gun crews loaded their guns. A few of the gunners were uneasy. They remembered the rush to equip the Armada with enough guns, and to train the gun crews. They knew the English were better trained, and had better guns of longer range.

As the first English gun shots thundered across the water, no one knew for sure how the battle would go. Never had two such large fleets of ocean going ships met in battle before. Never had ships been so heavily armed with guns.

Every man of the Spanish Armada knew he was on a sacred mission to restore England to the Catholic Church. But one or two of the commanders felt uneasy. They wondered if things would go according to plan. Even if Spain was victorious, would the expense have been worthwhile?

Armada battle.

The chessboard of Europe

Philip II of Spain (1556–1598) followed his father's advice "trust no one". He ran his empire almost singlehandedly, hardly leaving his monastery-palace, the Escorial, outside Madrid. As a result he was very overworked, and was often late in dealing with state matters. "If death came from Spain," joked one of his governors in Italy, "we should all live to a very great age." Philip was a Catholic and hated Protestantism. He dressed simply and hated vanity. He never blamed others for his own failures.

Philip was the most powerful Christian alive, ruling much of Europe. He wanted Europe to become a united Catholic empire and thought he was the best person to make this happen. He even

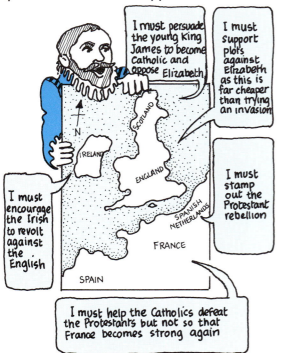

linked Spain to England when he married **Mary Tudor**, Elizabeth's elder sister, but she died in 1558.

Philip's main rival was France. Luckily for him, from 1562 the Catholics and Protestants of France started fighting each other, which left France unable to interfere in his plans. If the French Protestants won, France might then make an alliance with England. So Philip helped the French Catholics.

But Philip's main worry was how to defeat the Protestant rebels in the Netherlands, over which he was ruler. As the most powerful Catholic ruler, he could not allow them to challenge his authority. Nor could he afford to lose control of the Netherlands, because it was the main centre for northern Europe's trade.

Elizabeth I (1558–1603) relied on her advisers, taking praise if things went right but blaming them when things went wrong. She was irritable, cautious, but very clever. She knew it was important to be seen by her people and travelled all over her kingdom. She was a Protestant, but she did not mind some of her subjects being Catholic if they were loyal. She was vain, wore fine clothes and whitened her skin with egg white and powdered eggshell.

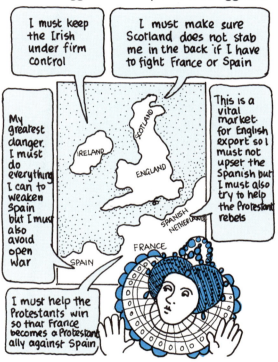

"Everything depends on the husband this woman takes," wrote one ambassador. Several rulers, including Philip, tried to join with England by marrying her. Elizabeth kept the choices open as long as possible. But if she had no children she would be followed as queen by her cousin **Mary Queen of Scots**, a Catholic. Mary was dangerous to Elizabeth. Catholics might try to kill Elizabeth to make Mary queen. Mary was driven out of Scotland and fled to England. Elizabeth dared not let her go; nor could she kill Mary in case this united Catholic Europe against her. So she kept Mary as a prisoner.

Most of England's trade with Europe went through the Spanish Netherlands. England wanted to support other Protestant countries but was afraid of upsetting Spain. Elizabeth could not decide which policy to follow and found herself doing both.

Things to find out and do

1. Here is Elizabeth's signature: try writing your own signature in this way with a nib pen or quill made from a feather.
2. Try making a simple version of Elizabeth's cosmetic recipe. Mix a little egg white with very finely powdered eggshell and powdered chalk. Rub some on your cheeks and see the effect.
3. Make a life-size collage of Philip.
4. Most European countries are mainly Catholic or Protestant. Which are which today?

Why Philip II decided to invade England

England was slowly dragged into Europe's religious struggle. The Pope (head of the Catholic church) declared Elizabeth a heretic, commanding Catholics to overthrow her. English Catholics were forced to choose between their queen and their religion. Philip began to help them against Elizabeth.

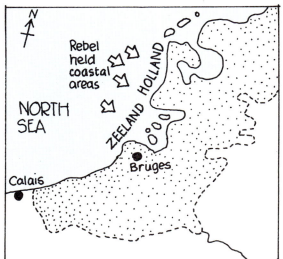

The Spanish Netherlands (present day Holland and Belgium).

Philip had been annoyed by English help to the Dutch and French Protestants. The Spanish army was the best in Europe, but fighting the Dutch rebels was costly and difficult. It had failed to recapture the coastal areas of Holland, mainly because the rebels got supplies from England. As Philip was helping her Catholic subjects, Elizabeth quietly sent the Dutch rebels more money and men.

A privateer captures a Spanish treasure ship.

Philip was also angry with English privateers which attacked his ships bringing gold and silver from America. These privateers were like pirate ships, but they had Elizabeth's approval. They even attacked Spanish ports in the Indies. Privateer expeditions were expensive and were paid for by merchants and nobles hoping to share in the plunder. When Philip complained, Elizabeth always had some excuse. But it was not long before he learned that Elizabeth and her advisers were also paying for these expeditions.

Philip now wanted to overthrow Elizabeth as well as the Dutch rebels. To do this he had to control the English Channel, but his fleet was not strong enough. Philip seized Portugal and took over its navy, which was better than his own. With it he hoped to master the English channel.

Then Elizabeth sent an official army to fight the Spanish in the Netherlands. She also sent her most famous privateer captain, **Francis Drake**, on a damaging raid to the Spanish Indies. This was an open declaration of war and Philip decided he must invade England without delay. He was further encouraged when Mary Queen of Scots named him heir to the English crown if she died before Elizabeth.

Elizabeth knew Philip planned to overthrow her. Mary was caught plotting her death with the support of Spain and some English Catholics. Elizabeth's advisers insisted that while Mary lived her own life would be in danger. They persuaded her to have Mary executed. When Philip heard the news, he obtained the Pope's support for his plan to remove Elizabeth and bring England back to the Catholic church. He had already started preparations to make this happen.

Mary's execution. Mary is shown three times in this picture. Try to spot them.

Things to find out and do

1. If you were Philip would you have decided to invade England? Do you think he had a good enough reason? Do you think he was wise to try?
2. Imagine what it was like as Elizabeth's prisoner for 19 years. If you were Mary what would you have done?
3. If you were Elizabeth would you have got involved with privateering and with the Dutch rebellion?

The sources of seapower

Traditional coastal navigation

Until the sixteenth century, sailors used special handwritten books called rutters which described the coastline to them, including how to enter harbours and avoid rocks or sandbanks.

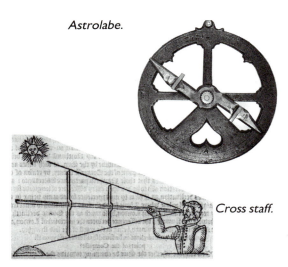

Astrolabe.

Cross staff.

Sailors could tell the depth of the sea by using a lead. This was a piece of lead with a hollowed out middle, filled with tallow (animal fat). It was lowered over the side of the ship and a sailor could feel the lead hit the sea bottom. The length of line let out told him the depth. The colour and texture of the sand which stuck to the tallow could be checked against what the rutter said about the seabed.

The new navigation

In the fifteenth century, sailors began to navigate out of sight of land, using mathematics, a compass and the stars and planets to help. The magnetic compass had been known in Europe since about 1000 AD but was now more widely used. A needle was magnetised by stroking it with a piece of magnetic iron ore, known as a lodestone. It was then fixed on a pivot to swing to a north-south position.

The fifteenth century navigators also learned to tell how far they were between the North and South Poles (latitude) by day or night. They used a cross staff by day, and an astrolabe by night to measure the angle between the horizon and the sun, or a known star. At night the Pole Star is always in the north, while the central stars of Orion's Belt are always due east and west.

8

It was harder for sailors to tell how far they had gone east or west (longitude). One way was a logline – a log of wood cast overboard on a line with knots in it at regular intervals. The speed of the ship was measured by the number of knots let out per minute. The captain would decide how far he had travelled, using his compass for direction, his logline for speed and his cross staff or astrolabe to check latitude.

Things to find out and do

1 Make your own compass. You need a magnet, a needle, scissors, paper or card, and the plastic plug from a Bic-type biro. Stroke the needle across the magnet ends in one direction only for about five minutes. Check if it has become magnetic. Push the needle through the Bic plug, just above the base. The needle must lie centrally across the base, and you may have to adjust it to find the point of balance so that it will swing. Cut out a circle from the card and mark it with the points of the compass. Sit the needle on the card and gently shake it to help the needle line up north to south. Find out which is north and which is south by checking against the sun (the sun travels from east to west and is due south at midday).

The wind is always described by the direction *from* which it is blowing; south, south south west (SSW), south west (SW), west south west (WSW), etc.

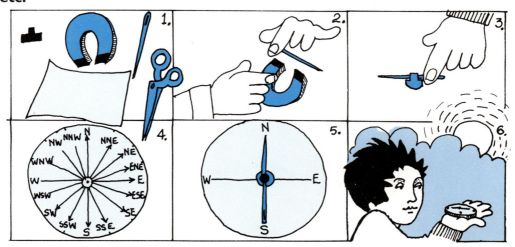

2 Draw a rutter of your home and street. Mark north on the rutter, making sure it is correctly aligned by using your compass.
3 Find the Pole Star and the central stars of Orion's Belt on a clear night.
4 Examine a globe or world map in an atlas and find the lines of latitude and longitude.

The sources of seapower

The development of ships

In the middle ages, ships were built for seaworthiness rather than speed. Even so, they were not really strong enough or large enough to travel far from the coast. They were often driven by oars as well as sail.

In the fifteenth century, new heavier ocean-going ships were developed. These ships enabled Columbus to sail to America in 1492, and Magellan to sail around the world, 1519–22. The biggest differences from the old ships were a dependence on sail only (instead of using oars) and the use of three masts instead of one. Without oars, fewer men were needed on board, which meant that food stores would last for longer. The three masts carried more sails to "catch" more wind, and therefore the new ships went faster. Sails were mainly square, but at the stern (rear) they had a lateen sail. This helped to prevent a cross wind from pushing the bows (front) of the ship off course.

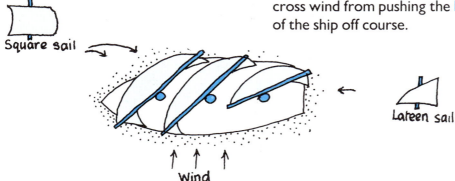

Warships had high wooden 'castles' at the bow and stern. Enemy ships sailed close to each other, and soldiers shot down from the castles before grappling and boarding the other ship. Their height made these ships slow, and less able to sail against the wind. A strong cross wind could blow a ship helplessly onto shore. The danger of capsizing could be lessened by filling the bottom of the ship with ballast, usually rocks and the ship's heavier stores. Even so, much of the ship stood out of the water and the body of the ship, the hull, could be blown along even without sails up.

Henry VIII's warship *Mary Rose* was an example of the dangers. It had many guns, and these fired out of gunports cut in the sides of the ship. The guns made it even more top-heavy. A sudden gust of wind tilted the *Mary Rose* so that the sea poured into the gunports on one side, and she capsized and sank.

The Mary Rose — a high-castled ship.

Things to find out and do

1 Design your own ships. You need some wine corks, cocktail sticks, paper, scissors and drawing pins. Slice the corks lengthways with a sharp knife. MIND YOUR FINGERS. These are your hulls. Stick broken cocktail sticks (masts) on the flat 'decks'. Cut out paper sails and fix. Stick drawing pins in the bottom of the hull as ballast. You can cut "tubby" or streamlined hulls. Experiment to discover which hull/ballast is most stable. Blow your ships *very* gently and steadily across a bowl of water.

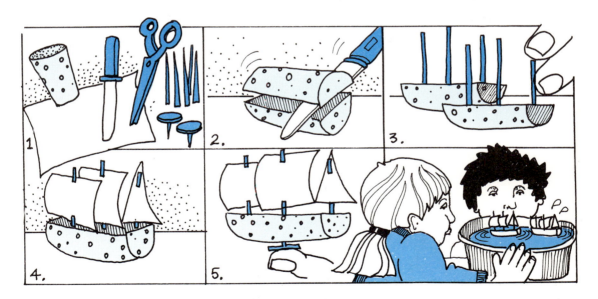

2 Look at the points of the compass on p. 9 and work out what all the initials mean. You will need to know them for plotting the course of the Armada.

3 The *Mary Rose* is preserved at Portsmouth. If you live near enough, ask your parents to take you to see it.

The new weapon of war: the gun

By 1588 armies still used swords and pikes (and even bows and arrows), but the most important weapon was increasingly the gun. Light guns, some handheld, were used to kill people. Heavier guns were used to batter, both on land and at sea.

Shot is fired from a gun by expanding gas. The gunpowder behind the shot explodes, heating the gas so that it expands very quickly. This pushes the shot out of the barrel at high speed. The principle is exactly the same with modern guns.

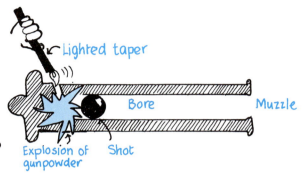

A gun was made by pouring hot metal into a mould. It had to be strong enough to throw a heavy shot for a reasonable distance. If it was not strong enough, it would blow up in the firer's face. A good brass gun was very expensive. It cost as much as it would cost to feed 800 soldiers for a month.

To hit a target a long way off the muzzle, or mouth, of a gun has to be raised, to allow for gravity. This is called elevation. Gunners had to learn how to judge the correct elevation to hit a target.

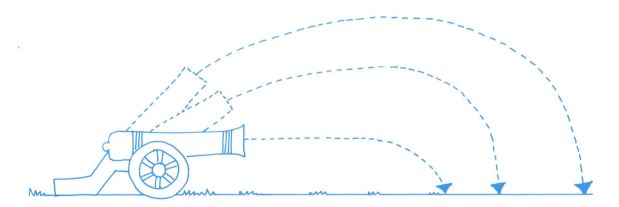

The use of gunports in the sides of ships made it possible to have more guns on lower decks. Warfare changed as ships began to rely on battering by gunfire as much as on grappling and boarding. The more a ship relied on its guns, the fewer soldiers it needed on board.

A fleet of faster ships could decide the distance at which a gun battle would take place. The best thing to do was to "hole" the enemy ship below the water line. This was difficult to do because, except at short range (say, 300 yards), ships' timbers were strong enough to resist shot. So guns were used to blow away the enemy's rigging (sails and ropes) and the woodwork on deck. Far more sailors were killed or injured by flying splinters than by the shot itself.

Things to find out and do

1 Guns, or artillery, are still divided into "batteries". Can you guess why the word "battery" is used?
2 If you live near enough, visit the Royal Artillery Museum in Woolwich.
3 Make your own gun. You need old kitchen roll or toilet roll tubes, small nails, sticky tape, small plastic bags (not bigger than 12" × 8") and a pingpong ball. Push the nail through the side of the roll, about half an inch from one end (to stop the ball rolling out of the tube). Stick the mouth of the plastic bag over the same end of the roll (just below the nail) with sticky tape, making it airtight. Roll the ball down the "barrel" till it stops on the nail. Blow down the barrel to inflate the bag with "gas". Rest the "gun" on the floor or table and "fire" by expelling the air from the bag. With a wedge (a cork) under the barrel you can adjust for range. With careful shooting you can judge whether the long (kitchen) or short (toilet) tubes make better guns. Have a competition with a friend to hit a target, an "enemy ship" on the far side of the room.

Life at sea

Life at sea could be hard, dangerous and uncomfortable. On a three month voyage, half the crew might die. They lived and slept below deck where it was dark except for a few oil lamps or candle lanterns. There was no ventilation, the smell was terrible and there was not enough fresh water to wash in.

Food was preserved in salt or dried, like salted meat and hardtack biscuits. Beer was thought safer to drink than water, though once it went off, it often upset the stomach. Each man was meant to get a pound of salted meat and a pound of biscuits daily, but he rarely did. When food barrels were opened, they were often rotten or had maggots. The crew often got diarrhoea and sickness. There were no toilets, just a few buckets below deck. Decks had to be swabbed (washed) down with salt water. The dirt washed down into the bottom of the ship, where it could infect the food still in barrels. Leather pumps would pump the dirt out, and also any sea water that leaked in. If the water pumped out was clean, it usually meant than the ship was holed.

Scurvy was the most common sickness apart from diarrhoea. It resulted from eating no fresh vegetables or fruit. The signs of scurvy were gumboils, tooth decay, sores and deep tiredness.

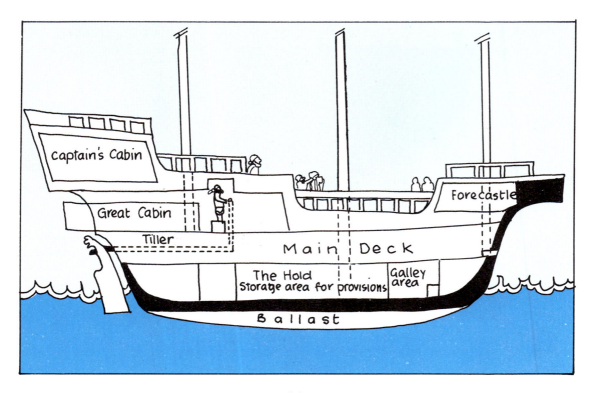

Discipline was often harsh. Sailors were frequently *flogged* (whipped). A sailor caught sleeping on watch more than 3 times was given a piece of bread, beer and a knife, and hung in a basket over the side of the ship. It was his choice whether to kill himself with the knife or cut the basket down and drown.

Why did men go to sea? Many were taken against their will, and some went because life for the poor was not very much better ashore. But others went for adventure and the chance to share in the spoils from a captured treasure ship.

Things to find out and do

1. Learn to tie a reef knot – used for *reefing* (rolling up) sails. Practise tying a *bowline* to make a loop that will not jam and a *sheet bend* (to connect 2 ropes of different thicknesses).

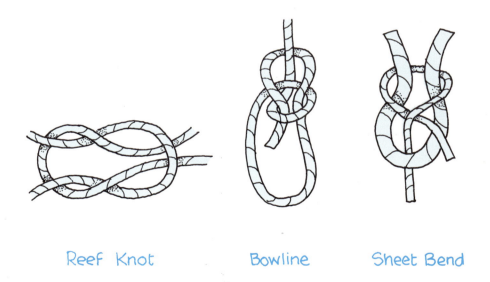

Reef Knot   Bowline   Sheet Bend

2. Make a genuine sea medicine, cinnamon water. You need one cinnamon stick (from a health shop). Boil it in 1 pint of water and allow it to cool. It was used to cure diarrhoea and sickness.
3. Imagine you are an ordinary sailor on an Elizabethan ship, keeping a diary of your voyage. Write an entry for one day to explain what your life is like.

The Armada plan: how it was made

The Army's plan Spanish commanders in the Netherlands had thought of invading England before. They believed their troops would be irresistible. In 1585 the **Duke of Parma**, Philip's nephew, planned to move about 30,000 men across the Channel in 800 barges. The problem was to protect the barges from enemy ships while crossing. He hoped to cross at night to gain total surprise. Philip wrote across this part of the plan "hardly possible!"

The Navy's plan Meanwhile, Philip's experienced admiral, **Santa Cruz**, offered to defeat England by sailing from Lisbon, destroying England's navy and landing an army. He wanted 550 ships, 30,000 sailors and 64,000 troops. Philip said it was far too expensive.

The Duke of Parma.

The Marquis of Santa Cruz.

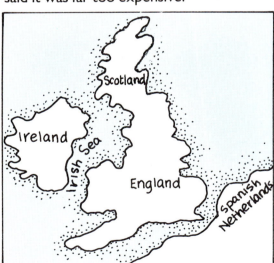

Philip's plan Philip made a new plan by putting the other two together. A smaller fleet — still bigger than any before it — would sail to the Netherlands, escort Parma's army across the Channel, and then turn to defeat the English navy.

However, Philip's plan had serious weaknesses:
1. Santa Cruz in Lisbon and Parma in the Netherlands were unable to speak directly with each other. Philip was the link between them. Letters took two weeks to get from Madrid to the Netherlands.
2. Philip decided to run the whole operation from his desk. He never visited the ports to inspect the ships, nor the Netherlands to inspect his army. He expected his orders to be carried out, even if his commanders thought they would not work.
3. The English fleet would try to stop the Armada linking up with Parma's troops. This link-up was the most dangerous part of Philip's plan.
4. Parma's barges were anchored in shallow water on the Netherlands coast. Because the Armada ships were so big, they could not sail close in to shore, but had to stay in deep water. This meant they could only protect the barges for a short distance across the Channel.
5. Finally, Philip ordered the Armada to sail up the *English* side of the Channel, leaving no chance of surprise.

Things to find out and do

1. Make your own Armada plan. Look at the map and consider how to invade. Irish Catholics might support a landing in Ireland, where there is only a small English army. But the Irish Sea has still to be crossed. West Scotland is still mainly Catholic and therefore a possibility. But the seas are much rougher up the west coast. A landing in the west of England and a march on London may be easier. Or do you prefer the army or navy plan?
2. Since Philip II, two other European leaders have planned to invade England with troop-filled barges from the Netherlands. Who were they?
3. If you were Philip, what would you have done about communication between Santa Cruz and Parma?
4. Imagine you are Parma and write to Philip pointing out the problems. Remember he is king and you must not offend him or suggest that he does not understand what he is doing.

The Spanish Armada

Philip assembled a fleet of 130 ships. Only 20 of these were real fighting galleons Their task was to protect the fleet and bear the brunt of any attack. There were also large merchant ships equipped with guns, and pinnaces, smaller ships used for carrying messages from ship to ship or to land. But the most defenceless were the cargo ships, carrying troops and stores for the invasion. These were slow and sat high out of the water.

The Armada's advantages It was to sail in disciplined formation and was organised in manageable squadrons. It was better at close fighting than the English fleet. It had more medium and short range cannon, and more soldiers to fight if an enemy ship could be boarded. "You must remember," warned Philip, "that the enemy's object will be to fight at long range, because of his advantage in artillery. The aim of our men must be to bring him to close quarters and grapple with him."

The Armada crescent formation.

The Armada's disadvantages To keep together, the fleet had to go at the speed of the slowest cargo ship. With its high castles and hulls, the Armada depended on favourable winds. Without these, it could be blown off course.

Things to find out and do

1 Test the problem of ballast and storage. Float a small tray or watertight box. Load it with "supplies" (stones, bits of wood, etc.), seeing how to arrange them best. Test what happens in a rough sea when the ship rolls. How would you prevent the cargo shifting in heavy seas?

2 Which do you think are more important, the Armada's advantages or disadvantages?

The English Fleet

From 1512, a Navy Office was set up to run the Navy properly. In 1577 **John Hawkins**, who had been a privateer captain like Drake, joined the Navy. Privateer ships were lighter and faster than galleons. Hawkins redesigned the Queen's ships to make them more like privateers. The basic naval tactic was to get upwind (the direction from which the wind is blowing) of the enemy, to be able to choose the moment of attack. Hawkins' improvements made sure the English fleet would be able to do this and shoot while staying out of range of the Spanish guns.

Things to find out and do

Make models of a Spanish high-castled ship and an English streamlined ship. You will need balsa wood, balsa cement or glue, plasticine, paperclips, cocktail or larger sticks and a sharp knife. Draw the shape of the hull on the balsa wood according to the length for width ratios. Cut out the hull. Cut out stern and bow blocks, making them higher for the Spanish ship. Fix the blocks onto the hull. Cut out and glue in the sides. Cut a slit in the bottom, push a slice of balsa wood through and weight it with plasticine. Use cocktail or larger sticks for the masts and make paper sails. Make a rudder and fix it on with a straightened out paperclip. Test the ships in a bowl of water and adjust the plasticine 'ballast' as necessary.

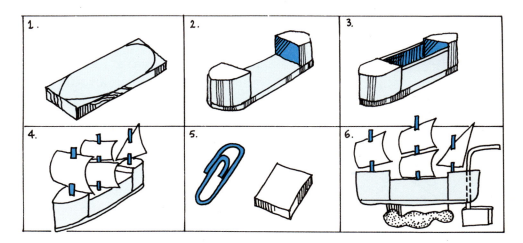

The battle of wits

Both sides used spies. Spain's spy network was organised by its ambassador in Paris, **Mendoza**. He had agents all over England, even in Elizabeth's court. Any spy who was caught knew he would be tortured to extract any information of value. A usual torture was the rack, which slowly tore the victim limb from limb. Spies could expect a terrible, slow and painful death.

Mendoza.

To put England off guard, Philip told Parma to keep peace talks with England going for as long as possible, but without making peace. Elizabeth was so anxious to avoid war she was still negotiating with Parma after the Armada had set sail.

In Spring 1587, Drake sailed on a secret mission. Mendoza knew about it within days but he was unsure of Drake's target. He asked the English ambassador, whom he paid well to let him read secret despatches from London. The ambassador (whose loyalty was suspected back in London) had been told that Drake was forbidden to enter any Spanish ports, and he said this to Mendoza. But Mendoza correctly guessed Drake's target was Cadiz, where a large Spanish fleet was at anchor. But his warning reached Philip too late, on the very day of Drake's attack.

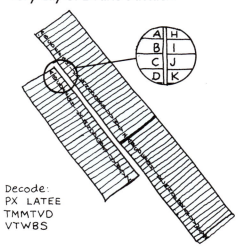

Decode:
PX LATEE
TMMTVD
VTWBS

Things to find out and do

1 One of Philip's secret messages was found inside a mirror. If you were a spy, where might you hide a message if you feared being searched?
2 Make your own spycode. Make two strips of paper, one 13 cm and the other 26 cm long. Mark them in ½ cm lengths. Write out the alphabet once on the shorter strip, twice on the longer strip. You can now encode a message.

The Cadiz Raid 1587

Drake had been attacking Spanish ships for twenty years, and his raids were legendary. The Spanish feared him and called him *El Draque*, the Dragon. On this occasion his task was simple, to disrupt the Armada's preparations so that it could not sail before the autumn storms. This would delay it till 1588.

Drake sailed into Cadiz harbour late one April afternoon, achieving complete surprise. For a day and a half his ships pounded the Spanish fleet, till he had sunk at least 24 ships. On the Portuguese coast he captured ships carrying seasoned wood for making airtight barrels in which food and water would be stored. They were meant for the Armada, which would now have to store food and water in unseasoned barrels. This meant food was more likely to go rotten, and water more likely to leak. Drake kept raiding the coastline till June. On his way home he captured a ship laden with spices, silks, gold and silver worth far more than the ships he had sunk at Cadiz.

Drake's mission was highly successful. Philip had to postpone the invasion. He took the bad news calmly, noting "The loss was not very great, but the daring was very great indeed". Drake himself described it as "singeing (burning) the King of Spain's beard".

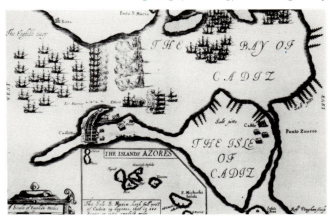

Drake's fleet entering Cadiz harbour.

Things to find out and do

1 Drake's raid took him to Cadiz, Cape St Vincent, Lagos, Sagres, Cape St Vincent, Sagres, the Azores and back to Plymouth. Plot his voyage on an atlas map of Spain and Portugal.
2 Which ship did Drake sail around the world in, 1577–80?

The Armada sets sail

When Santa Cruz died early in 1588, the **Duke of Medina Sidonia**, Spain's senior duke, was made commander of the Armada. He had never commanded a single ship let alone a fleet. He was intelligent and brave but knew that experience was essential. He suggested that someone else should be commander, but Philip would not listen, So he did his best, taking with him Spain's most experienced seamen to give him advice.

There was a great scramble to get things ready in time. There was a shortage of guns and trained gunners. There had been a lot of illness among the seamen and much food was rotten. When the Armada

The Duke of Medina Sidonia.

sailed at last from Lisbon on 30 May 1588, things continued to go wrong. A strong north west wind at first blew it south towards Cape St Vincent. By tacking (zigzagging across the wind) it could just sail slowly northwards, but sheltered from the stormy weather at Corunna on 19 June. Ships were damaged, food was rotten and water barrels leaked. Hundreds of men had diarrhoea.

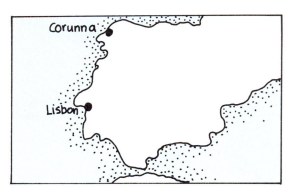

Tacking.

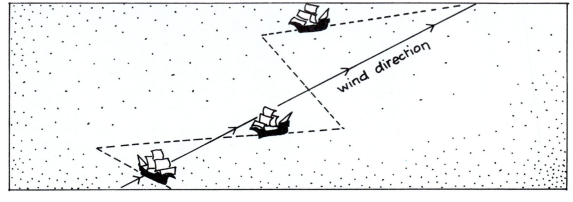

The Armada was not able to sail again until 22 July. Three days later, Medina Sidonia sent a pinnace to warn Parma to be ready with his army and barges. On 29 July he sighted the Lizard in Cornwall, and sent another ship to Parma. He was worried that he had not heard from Parma. He also wrote to Philip 'Without information from Parma I can only advance slowly.... all along the Netherlands there is no harbour to shelter and I may be driven onto the sandbanks and destroyed."

Parma had been ready a year earlier, but since then he had lost interest in the invasion. Disease and *desertion* had reduced his army to 17,000 men, and his barges were unseaworthy. He saw the faults in Philip's plan, and decided he would not sail until the sea was dead calm and the English fleet had been chased away. He told Philip this, but Philip had not told Medina Sidonia. Parma was determined to avoid putting to sea and getting the blame when things went wrong. So he simply did not reply to the Armada's messages.

Things to find out and do

1 Ships mainly communicated with each other by shouting, but they also used flags and guns at greater distances. Think what orders you might want to give as commander, and design and make paper flags to get these orders carried out. You should also make a flag for other ships to say "signal received".
2 Things were clearly going wrong for the Armada. Who was to blame, or was it just bad luck? List what you think Philip, Medina Sidonia and Parma could each be blamed for.
3 How would you have put things right?

Defending England by sea

Lord Howard of Effingham, the Lord Admiral, was chosen like Medina Sidonia, because he was a nobleman. But he had had time to study seamanship and work closely with Hawkins and Drake, who was made his vice-admiral.

Lord Howard of Effingham.

Howard, in his flagship, the *Ark Royal*, had sailed from Margate to join Drake in Plymouth on 2 June. Together they had about 90 ships, with another 40 off Dover. Elizabeth wanted the fleets to patrol the Channel. Howard and Drake wanted to

The Ark Royal.

attack the Armada in Spanish waters, but did not know whether the Armada had set sail. When they learnt the Armada was in Corunna, they sailed on 4 July with a north east wind, hoping to attack it in port. But the wind kept on changing. On 20 July, when the English were only 60 miles from the Spanish coast, it blew strongly from the south, ideal for the Armada to reach England. Fearing it might pass them unseen, the English fleet sailed hard for England, reaching Plymouth on 22 July.

Plymouth Sound.

At 3pm on 29 July a pinnace sailed into Plymouth having sighted the Armada off the Scilly Isles. Drake was playing bowls when the news came, but there was no hurry. The English fleet could not get out of Plymouth Sound until the tide turned at 10pm.

Things to find out and do

1 Do you think Drake and Howard were right in wishing to attack the enemy fleet in its own waters? Or was the risk of missing the Armada too great?
2 Cut off the Operations Map on the back cover and follow the instructions.

Defending England by land

A system of beacons (bonfires) had been arranged on the hills and headlands across the south coast of England as an early warning system. As the Armada came into view on 30 July, the beacons were lit. They carried the message faster than any horseman eastwards as far as Kent and Essex, and northwards across the country. By the following morning not only London but York and Durham knew the Spaniards were coming.

At the sound of church bells, able-bodied men assembled at town square or village green to form militias, or armed bands. They were poorly armed and hardly a match for the Spanish infantry (foot soldiers). Some sneaked off home when no-one was looking. In London, an army was assembled on the north bank of the Thames at Tilbury, to defend the capital.

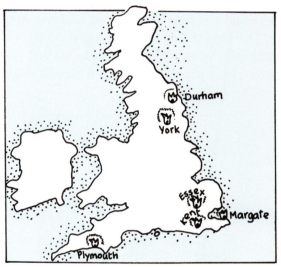

Things to find out and do

1 Mark the location of the main English army on your Operations Map.
2 Work out a beacon system with a friend, using torches. Decide on signals for "danger alert", "enemy landing", and "relax, danger has passed".
3 Ask grandparents, or anyone you know over sixty, to tell you what they remember of the Home Guard during the Second World War. Would a beacon system have been used if Germany had invaded England in 1940?

Battles in the Channel

The two fleets saw each other properly for the first time at dawn on 31 July. Both had an unpleasant shock. A west north west wind was blowing, so the Armada hoped to hold the advantage by being upwind of the English. This would allow it to choose the moment of attack. But during the night most of the English fleet had sailed around the Armada to be west of it by dawn. The Spanish realised that, against such nimbleness, they had no hope of cornering and boarding the English ships.

The English hoped to attack and batter individual ships in the Armada. But they saw that the Armada was sailing in a tight crescent-shaped formation with its strongest ships along the outer edge. If the English attacked the weakest point (the rear) too

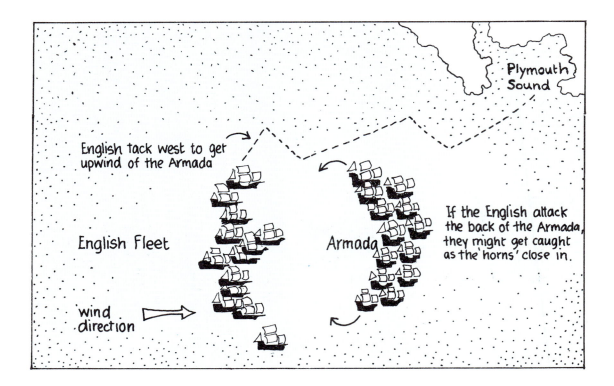

closely, the "horns" of the Spanish crescent might move together, enclosing them and preventing escape. They would just have to follow the Armada, hoping to cripple it by gunfire and pouncing on stragglers.

The following day the English captured two ships. One had accidentally blown up and the other had lost a mast in an accidental collision with another Spanish ship. But English gunfire had done almost no damage at all.

On 2 August the wind changed to the north east for a few hours. This gave the Armada a chance to corner some English ships at Portland Bill, but the English were too quick. The English guns shot further and faster than the Spanish ones but did no serious damage. Over half Howard's ammunition had gone. He feared the Armada might seize the Isle of Wight and the Solent anchorage. Only hot pursuit would keep it moving, so he asked for urgent supplies of ammunition from nearby ports. "Let us have with some speed some great shot sent us of all bigness," he wrote, "for this service will continue long; and some powder with it."

The battle of Portland Bill.

Medina Sidonia was also running low on ammunition but he had more important worries too. He sent Parma another message, "Send someone urgently, bring replies to my questions, and send me pilots (guides) for the coast, without which I do not know where I can find shelter for such large ships in case I am overtaken by bad weather. Also send me powder, shot, and small boats fast enough to grapple and board the English fleet." He did not know that Parma had no such boats available. He thought for a moment of seizing the Isle of Wight but remembered Philip had strictly forbidden this.

Things to find out and do

1 Continue to plot the movements on your Operations Map. Use the information from the maps to help you.
2 Imagine yourself first as Howard, then as Medina Sidonia. Would you have acted differently and if so, why?

The defeat of the Armada

Medina Sidonia halted the Armada off Calais late on 6 August. He could not take his ships into either Calais or Gravelines because they were French ports. Dunkirk was too shallow and Ostend was held by the English. Next morning he learned that Parma's army would not be ready for a week. Now he faced disaster, anchored on an exposed coastline with a strong tidal flow, dangerous sandbanks to the north east and the English fleet to the west.

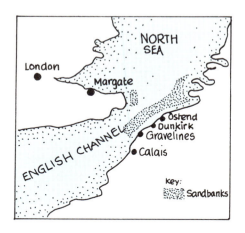

Howard had decided to keep the Armada moving. Just before midnight on 7 August, as the tide turned to flow eastwards, he sent eight fireships floating towards the Armada. The Spanish had no more than 15 minutes to cut anchor cables and sail off. Thanks to good discipline not a single ship was burnt or wrecked, but the Armada formation was ruined. Early next morning, Spanish ships were drifting helplessly ten or more miles east along the coast. The wind had swung from south west to almost north north west, threatening to blow them onto the Dutch sandbanks.

Medina Sidonia with his best ships regained formation in time to meet the English attack from the west. This time, the English sailed much closer, to within 200 yards. Their guns were able to smash holes in the Spanish ships, four of which were sunk that day. By late afternoon, Medina Sidonia had run out of shot but did not know that the English had run out too. He had a far greater worry on his mind. The whole Armada was about to be shipwrecked on the Dutch sandbanks.

Through the night and morning of 9 August, the Spanish worked to stay afloat. The pumps on damaged ships worked non-stop. Shot holes were repaired with sheets of lead. Each ship anxiously measured the depth of the sea and prayed for a change of wind that would take them off the sandbanks. At midday, as they gave up all hope, the wind suddenly changed to south west, blowing the Armada northwards.

Medina Sidonia held a meeting with his captains. They had no ammunition and could not sail against the wind. They had no choice but to sail northwards, driven by the wind. It was the end of the Armada's mission.

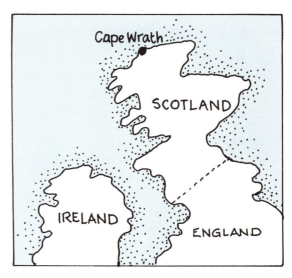

Medina Sidonia gave strict orders to avoid the coasts of Scotland and Ireland. But his chief worries were early autumn storms and the shortage of food. Everyone went onto half rations. About 22 August, the Armada passed Cape Wrath, where storms worse than anyone could remember scattered the Armada in different directions. It never came together again.

Many ships sank in heavy seas. At least 26 ships were driven onto the Irish coast, where cannon and other remains are still found. Survivors crawling ashore were robbed by local people and killed by the English troops.

On 23 September, Medina Sidonia's ship reached Spain and Philip learnt for the first time the true and terrible story of the Armada's ordeal.

Things to find out and do

1 Continue to plot events on your Operations Map.
2 Try living on Armada starvation rations, half a pound of hardtack biscuits. These were made of flour and water. You may use the same weight of water biscuits.
3 Look up the tides in today's newspaper and check when it is high tide today. How often does the tide change in every 24 hours?
4 Imagine you are a journalist and write a headline and short report of what happened to the Armada (1) for a Spanish newspaper and (2) for an English newspaper.

The day of reckoning

Philip II accepted the Armada defeat as God's will. He did not blame Medina Sidonia but the rest of Spain did. The whole thing cost Philip half the yearly amount of money needed for running the Spanish empire.

Spanish losses
Cost in ships: approximately 60 ships lost.
Cost in lives: probably 20,000 out of 30,000 dead. Of these, 1,500 died in battle, 6,000 died by shipwreck but most died from disease. Many died after reaching Spain.

England's losses
Not a single ship was lost and only 150 men died in the fighting. But hundreds of others died of disease. On one ship alone, 200 out of the 500 crew died. In Margate, Admiral Howard saw other sailors collapse and die in the streets. "It would grieve a man's heart to see them that had served so valiantly to die so miserably."

But England rejoiced and a commemorative medal was struck. Around it in Latin were the words "God blew and they were scattered."

The following year Drake took 150 ships to capture Lisbon, but it was almost as big a disaster as the Armada had been. Thousands of men died. Philip made two more attempts to invade England in 1596 and 1597 but both failed because of stormy weather. Elizabeth spent a fortune on the defence of England, and the war only ended when Elizabeth died in 1603.

Things to find out and do

1 Design your own Armada medal on paper. Try making it in clay.
2 If you were Medina Sidonia, how would you have felt when you got back to Spain? Would you blame anyone – the English, Philip, Parma or yourself?
3 If you were Elizabeth how would you have dealt with the continued Spanish threat? Use your Operations Map and mark where you would keep ships and troops to defend England. Or do you think it better to try for a peace agreement? If so, what would you offer Spain?

If the Armada had landed

Parma was to land his army at Margate, which was undefended, and march on London to take Elizabeth prisoner. Only two cities, Canterbury and Rochester, lay between Margate and London. Neither had walls strong enough to resist Parma's seige artillery. Parma's infantry would have captured them both easily. Sir Roger Williams, who had fought Parma in the Netherlands, said, "To speak troth (truth), no Armie that ever I saw passes that of the Duke de Parma for discipline and good order." At Dover, members of the Kent militia ran away then they saw the size of the Armada on the horizon.

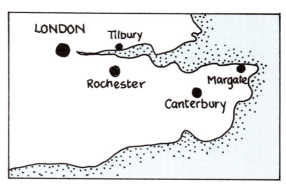

Parma might well have beaten Elizabeth's army and entered London. Philip might have made his daughter queen. England could have become Catholic again, and part of the Spanish empire.

Elizabeth made a fiery speech to her army of 10,000 assembled at Tilbury:

I am resolved, in the midst and heat of battle, to live or die amongst you all, and to lay down for my God and for my kingdom and for my people, my honour and my blood, even in the dust. I know I have the body of a weak and feeble woman, but I have the heart and stomach of a king, and a king of England too, and think foul scorn that Parma or Spain, or any prince of Europe should dare invade the borders of my realm.

Things to find out and do

1 Check where Tilbury is on the map. If you were uncertain where Parma might land, where would you assemble your army?
2 Elizabeth made her famous speech on 19 August. Where was the Armada then?

Armada Crossword

Across

1. Our sovereign lady in 1588 and 1988
8. He got the English fleet ready
10. The Spanish commander in the Netherlands
11. Islands, East and West, from which Spain brought back riches
13. El Draque in English
14. Half the Armada commander's name
15. Measurement of speed, tied in a logline

Down

2. The wind that blew the Armada towards the sandbanks
3. The first bit of England the Armada sighted
4. The English fleet defeated it
5. Elizabeth's troops cheered her to the . . . . .
6. The English commander
7. Philip's rank
9. What you hope your ship won't do
12. What the Armada crossed

Answers

Across 1 Queen Elizabeth 8 Hawkins 10 Parma 11 Indies 13 Dragon 14 Medina 15 Knot
Down 2 NNW 3 Lizard 4 Armada 5 Echo 6 Howard 7 King 9 Sink 12 Sea

ISBN 0 340 40892 8

First published 1987

Copyright © 1987 David McDowall

All rights reserved. No part of this publication may be reproduced or transmitted in any form or by any means, electronic or mechanical, including photocopy, recording, or any information storage and retrieval system, without permission in writing from the publisher.

Typeset in Gill medium by Gecko Ltd, Bicester, Oxon.

Printed in Great Britain for Hodder and Stoughton Educational, a division of Hodder and Stoughton Ltd, Mill Road, Dunton Green, Sevenoaks, Kent by Stoneford Press Ltd, Northfleet, Kent